PLACES OF ❖ WORSHIP

Hindu Temples

Rasamandala Das

Heinemann
LIBRARY

First published in Great Britain by Heinemann Library
Halley Court, Jordan Hill, Oxford OX2 8EJ
a division of Reed Educational and Professional Publishing Ltd.
Heinemann is a registered trademark of Reed Educational & Professional Publishing Limited.

OXFORD MELBOURNE AUCKLAND
BLANTYRE IBADAN JOHANNESBURG
GABORONE PORTSMOUTH (NH) USA CHICAGO

Designed by Tinstar Design
Illustrations by Nicholas Beresford-Davies and Martin Griffin
Printed by Wing King Tong in Hong Kong

02 01 00 99
10 9 8 7 6 5 4 3 2 1

British Library Cataloguing in Publication Data

Das, Rasamandala
   Hindu temples. - (Places of worship)
   1. Temples, Hindu - Juvenile literature
   I. Title
   294.5'35

ISBN 0 431 05182 8
This book is also available in a hardback library edition (ISBN 0 431 05177 1).

Acknowledgements

The Publishers would like to thank the following for permission to reproduce photographs:
Andes Press Agency/Carlos Reyes-Manzo, pp. 5, 8, 13, 16, 18, 20; Circa Photo Library/John Smith, p. 21; Das, Rasamandala, p. 6; Emmett, Phil & Val, pp. 7 (both), 9, 10, 11 (both), 12, 14, 17, 19; Pro-Colour Lab, p. 4.

Cover photograph reproduced with permission of Phil and Val Emmett.

Our thanks to Philip Emmett for his comments in the preparation of this book, and to Louise Spilsbury for all her hard work.

Every effort has been made to contact copyright holders of any material reproduced in this book. Any omissions will be rectified in subsequent printings if notice is given to the Publisher.

Contents

Words printed in **bold letters like these**
are explained in the Glossary.

What is a temple?

A temple is a building where **Hindus** come to worship. Hindus follow the religion called **Hinduism**, which comes from India. Hinduism is the oldest religion in the world. It goes back more than 5000 years.

An Indian word for temple is **mandir**. A mandir is a special place where Hindus can feel close to **God**.

Some Hindu temples are small and simple. Others, like this one, are large and often covered with beautiful carvings. Large, old temples, like this one, are usually found in India.

Hindu people in Britain

Many Hindus have come to Britain over the last 50 years. Some came from India. Others moved to Britain from East Africa.

When Hindu people first came to Britain most of them were not very rich. They could not afford to build their own temples. They bought old buildings and turned them into temples.

Many Hindus moved from India and East Africa to Britain.

Britain

India

East Africa

This temple is in South London. It was one of the first to be opened in Britain. The building used to be a church.

Temples in Britain

There are many different types of **mandir**. Some are in the town and some in the countryside. Some are old buildings, some are new ones.

This temple has a small farm with bulls and cows. The farm provides food and milk for the temple.

Orange flags

In Britain, many **Hindu** temples look just like other buildings. You can tell what they are by the orange flag that often flies from the roof.

New temples

Hindu people in Britain have begun to build their own mandirs. Some new temples are built to look like old Hindu temples in India. Others are built in a modern style.

This modern temple is in Leicester.

Where to find Hindu temples

There are over 150 temples in Britain. Most Hindu people live around London or Leicester. Others live around Birmingham, Manchester and other large cities and towns.

This mandir is in North London. It looks like some of the temples in India and is made from marble.

What's inside?

Visitors to the temple take off their shoes before going in. This is to show respect and to keep the temple clean. There are special racks to put your shoes on.

When you enter the temple you may notice the smell of **incense**. Incense is a perfume which is burned to make a pleasant scent.

There are often many rooms in a **mandir**. There are usually offices, a kitchen and a dining area, as well as a room for **worship**.

Worshippers remove their shoes before going into a temple.

The temple room

When Hindus enter the main temple room they ring a bell hanging from the ceiling. Then they stand in front of a **shrine** and offer prayers to the **murtis**. The murtis are sacred **images** of the Hindu **gods** and **goddesses** inside the shrine.

After praying, worshippers leave gifts of money, rice, fruit or flowers for the gods and goddesses in the shrine. Then they may sip a few drops of **holy water**.

A Hindu woman offers prayers to a shrine. You can see the gifts of flowers in front of the murtis.

The shrine

Only **priests** are allowed into the **shrine** itself.
The priests look after the **murtis** with love and
devotion. They clean and dress them each morning.
You cannot usually see this because the curtains in
front of the shrine are closed at such times.

Priests also offer the murtis **vegetarian** food.
After it has been offered to the murtis, it is
called **prashad**. This **holy** food is given to visitors.

This priest is **worshipping** murtis in the temple shrine.

God, gods and goddesses

Hindus worship many different murtis. Some are thought to be **God**. Others are lesser **gods** and **goddesses**. Hindus believe they have great power over the universe.

There are three main gods and goddesses: **Vishnu**, **Shiva** and **Durga**. **Krishna** is another name for Vishnu. You can see him on page 10. He is often shown playing a flute.

A painting of Shiva carrying a trident, drum and water pot.

Shiva's wife is called Durga. In this murti she is shown riding a lion.

Worship in the temple

In the temple, some people **worship** alone. Most take **darshan**, which is when they stand before the **murtis** and offer prayers. They may also chant **mantras**, counting them on a string of beads. A mantra is a short prayer which is said again and again.

The arti ceremony

Some worship is performed in groups. The most important ceremony is called **arti**. A lamp, a flower, **incense** and water are offered to the murti. The lamp and the flower are then passed around the **congregation**.

The arti lamp is passed around worshippers, who either stand or sit cross-legged on the floor.

Other types of worship

There are other ways **Hindus** worship together.
One is the **sacred-fire ceremony**. It is often
performed at special events, such as weddings.
(You can see a picture of this ceremony on page 18.)

Listening to readings from the **holy** books is another
form of worship. Hindus have many different holy
books. The oldest are called the **Vedas**. For many
Hindus the **Bhagavad Gita** (The Song of **God**) is the
most important.

Holy books

Some Hindu holy books
praise God, some tell
people how to worship,
and others are about
Hindu beliefs. Many
of them are written
in **Sanskrit**.

A **priest** talking to
people in a temple
in Southall, London.

Festivals

The temple is very busy on festival days. There are many festivals during the year. For most **Hindus**, the main one is **Divali**, the Hindu New Year. At Divali the temple is decorated with rows of candles or lights.

At most festivals special stories are told. There is music, singing and dancing. It is a time for fun and celebration.

Girls and women perform a stick-dance during the **Navaratri** festival.

Festival food

On many festivals Hindus **fast**. This means that they go without food for some time. This is followed by feasting. Most food eaten at festivals is **vegetarian**.

Janmashtami is a festival that celebrates **Krishna's** birthday. On this day some Hindus fast until midnight, when Krishna was born. Then there is a beautiful **arti** ceremony followed by a feast.

Festival food

Here are just a few of the special foods eaten at Hindu festivals: puris are flat round breads fried in ghee (oil made from butter); samosas are pastries stuffed with vegetables; burfi is a kind of fudge made from sugar and milk.

These Hindu women are preparing festival food in a temple kitchen.

Music and art

Music is very important to **Hindus**. Hindu songs of **worship** are called **bhajans**. They are sung during the **arti** ceremony and at festivals. They are often sung in **Hindi** or another Indian language.

These are the main instruments played during festivals or worship. Tablas are drums you play with the hands. Hand cymbals are used to keep the rhythm (beat). The harmonium is a small organ pumped by hand.

Hindu musicians playing during a wedding celebration. You can see the tablas (drums) in the left of the picture.

Temple pictures

In a Hindu temple you can see paintings or pictures of the different **gods** and **saints**. They are very brightly coloured. You will also see different **symbols** connected with **Hinduism**.

Hindu symbols

This symbol is called **Aum**. It represents Hinduism. You say the word as if it were written 'Ah-oo-m'.

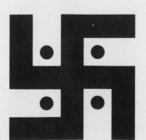

This is a swastika. It is a sign of good luck.

This is a picture of the god **Ganesha**. He has an elephant's head. He is the son of **Shiva**.

We listen to music with our ears. We see pictures with our eyes. Can you find out how Hindus use their nose, tongue and sense of touch in worship?

You can find the answers on page 23.

The temple and the people

The temple is not just for **worship**. It is also a place where **Hindus** meet together for fun, celebrations and to help others.

Many Hindu families use the temple for special events. These include weddings and the name-giving ceremony for babies.

The **sacred-fire ceremony** performed during a wedding at a mandir.

Some events are performed outside the temple, often at home. For these ceremonies, such as funerals, the **priest** comes from the **mandir**.

Helping others

In Britain, the temple is also a **community** centre. Rooms are used for meetings and for teaching. There may be a large hall for putting on Indian music, dance and theatre. The building is used as a base to assist the poor, old people and others who need help. Some temples help feed the homeless.

Hindus believe that special care should be given to children, women, animals (especially cows), **holy** people and old people. Hindus believe that if these five groups are cared for God will be pleased and everyone will be happy.

This dance in Leicester is part of a charity event.

The home as a temple

Hindus believe that the home should also be a temple. Every Hindu house has its own **shrine**. This may simply be a few pictures on a shelf. Sometimes it may take up a whole room. The shrine usually has **images** or pictures of one or more of the **gods** and **goddesses**.

In **Hinduism** there is no special day of the week for **worship**. Hindus usually worship at least once a day. Early morning before dawn is thought to be the best time. It is very calm and peaceful then.

A Hindu family worshipping at a shrine in their home.

Learning about Hinduism

Hindu children learn by taking part in worship at home. They may help their parents during the **arti** ceremony.

Children also learn by hearing stories from their parents or grandparents. Sometimes when they are playing they may even pretend to be **Krishna**, **Shiva** or **Durga**. By remembering **God**, the home also becomes a temple. It is a very special place.

Sometimes Hindu children have their own small shrines. Here a Hindu girl is praying to Krishna.

Glossary

The letters in brackets help you to say each word.

arti (ar-tee) main ceremony in Hindu temples

Aum (om) symbol which is often used to represent Hinduism

Bhagavad Gita (buh-guh-vud gee-tuh) one of the most important and popular Hindu holy books

bhajan (buh-juhn) Hindu song of worship; a song in praise of God

community a group of people; the people who live in the neighbourhood

congregation the group of people who come to the church, mosque or temple

darshan (dar-shun) coming before the murti; seeing the murti

Divali (dee-var-lee) one of the main Hindu festivals. For most Hindus it is the New Year celebration.

Durga (doo-r-guh) the main Hindu goddess; the wife of Shiva

fast to go without food for some time for religious reasons

Ganesha (gun-esh) a Hindu god. One of the sons of Shiva and Durga.

God the Greatest person; the highest of the gods. Krishna (or Vishnu) is often thought to be God, and sometimes Shiva.

god a male being believed to have great power over human lives

goddess a female being believed to have great power over human lives

Hindi the main official language of India

Hinduism the main religion of India

Hindus followers of the religion of Hinduism

holy means respected because it is to do with God

holy water water which has been specially blessed

image picture or holy statue of a god or goddess

incense perfume which is burned to make a pleasant smell

Janmashtami (juhn-mush-tuh-mee) Hindu festival held on Krishna's birthday

Krishna (krish-nuh) one of the main Hindu gods

mandir (mun-deer) Indian word for temple

mantra (mun-truh) prayer; a string of holy words

murti (moo-r-tee) a form or image of a god or goddess usually made of wood, metal or marble

Navaratri (nuh-vuh-ruh-tree) festival held in honour of Durga. It lasts for nine days.

prashad (pruh-shard) sacred food; food offered to God

priests people who lead worship

sacred-fire ceremony Hindu ceremony where grains are thrown into a fire

Sanskrit (sann-skrit) very old language once spoken in India

saint someone who lives an especially good religious life

Shiva (shiver) one of the main Hindu gods

shrine holy place where people worship

symbol sign with a special meaning

Vedas (vay-duhs) the oldest Hindu holy books. They contain the basic truths which Hindus believe never change.

vegetarian food which does not have meat in it

Vishnu (vish-noo) one of the main Hindu gods

worship show respect and love for God, saints or anything which is holy

Answers to questions on page 17:
Hindus use the nose to smell the **incense** and flowers offered to God. The tongue is used to taste **prashad**. The sense of touch is used when chanting on meditation beads.

Index